Chocolate Covered

FRENCH
FRIES

A Recipe
for Any
Relationship

KEVIN
KISHOR

Chocolate Covered French Fries
Copyright © 2020 by Kevin Kishor

All rights reserved. No part of this publication may be reproduced, distributed, or transmitted in any form or by any means, including photocopying, recording, or other electronic or mechanical methods, without the prior written permission of the author, except in the case of brief quotations embodied in critical reviews and certain other non-commercial uses permitted by copyright law.

Tellwell Talent
www.tellwell.ca

ISBN
978-0-2288-2618-7 (Paperback)
978-0-2288-2619-4 (eBook)

Table of Contents

Introduction:
"Chocolate-Covered French Fries?" v

Chapter 1: #1 Rule: It's All About You 1
Chapter 2: Unsubtle Subtlety 10
Chapter 3: The Art of Giving and Receiving 18
Chapter 4: Valuable Foundations? 27
Chapter 5: Passionfruit 36
Chapter 6: Bitcoin That Lasts! 44

Epilogue:
Rowing like Chris Rock 53

Introduction:

"CHOCOLATE-COVERED FRENCH FRIES?"

The title of this book was inspired by my "middle" daughter, just as so much of this book was inspired by my other children since it is all about relationships. I have deliberately chosen to highlight that she is the "middle" daughter because we know that birth placement, like it or not, plays a major factor in how she relates to the family and others in the world. I used her question for the title because it came up in a random conversation one day that she and I were having. She asked if I've ever had, would try, or have heard of chocolate-covered French fries. I thought to myself, wow, what a strange concept: pairing two foods together that on their own can be so great (depending on who you talk to), but together could be potentially delicious or disgusting. For some reason, this idea made me draw parallels to relationships. It is true that two people of any type on their own can be great, but combining them with others could either be disastrous or a beautiful masterpiece!

This parallel could be a stretch, but hopefully it has gotten you interested enough to read. If you are like me, a book's Introduction is the part you often skip. The concept of grabbing people's attention in a book's Introduction also closely resembles an initial aspect of relationships. In the beginning, it often happens that one person tries, or both people try, to stand out from others in hopes of securing their attraction, especially if the potential for romance exists. This can also be applied to others like a child trying to stand out from their siblings or classmates, or an employee trying to stand out from other co-workers and so on.

Unfortunately, what often follows is a plateau or an underwhelming experience — it does not sustain — but we can't overgeneralize this, of course. So, my hope is that this Introduction does not just get your attention and then lack lustre later in the book(s). The usual goal of my writing is to be as practical as possible in a way that can apply to as many types of relationships as we may experience in our lives. But first, let me tell you a little about me and the motivations for this book.

I am the oldest of three children. The other two are sisters, and one is a half-sister but a sister all the same to me. Those dynamics, roles, and birth placements impact who I am today. I was born into a huge extended mixed-Guyanese family which at the time I was born they had pretty much all recently moved to Canada, the U.S., and Europe. I am thankful to be born a Canadian. My parents only lasted a couple of years in their marriage, which was complicated as are all; they were divorced before I made it to kindergarten so I don't remember much. I won't be addressing their situation since it is not the focus here; however, it of course has impacted my life and indirectly this book too. Nonetheless, our large and diverse extended family influenced and continues to influence many of my decisions in life. I am not ashamed of that because it is part of my cultural heritage to be close to my family and find Value in the good and the crazy too!

The first major impact my family had on my adult life was the decision to study Religious, Social, and Cultural History as my first degree in the Arts. Looking back, I realized that having all types of religious representation in the family — from Catholics, to Hindus, to Jehovah's Witnesses, to Pentecostals — helped stir my fascination with how so many people from the same family could have such different beliefs. I figured I needed to find a way to love all these people regardless.

My thinking was that "understanding" them was the best path to try. Throughout this book, I highlight certain key Ingredients for creating our Recipes with an *. Here is the first... when people tell you that Love is "understanding," they are lying to you or they are at least misguided. If Love requires us to understand the actions of others, then we will never get there since on most days we can't even understand ourselves. Although Love is complex, it is not a feeling, and Love is definitely NOT understanding, either. Love is more likely *Acceptance**. However, Acceptance does NOT mean condoning bad behaviour; let's be clear on that.

I am grateful to many people who encouraged me. Some even challenged me to write this book, like one friend who I consider dear and timely (thank you, Sien). As for everyone else, I hope you know who you are too! A special shout-out to Kamar Burke: you have been such a brother to me through everything; thank you. Also, I want to give special credit to former journalist and my cousin, Rene Khodai. He dared to take on the responsibility of reading the first drafts of this adventure of mine. You see, I was hesitant to put myself out there like this since I have experienced some major "failures," changes, or hardships in my personal relationships. I need to be honest: I had a great fear of being capable or qualified enough to publish an original work — despite of all my years of studies and coaching families. My biggest doubts lie in the fact that my marriage of almost half my adult life "failed" or came to an end a few years before writing this book.

The ending of my marriage is ironic because I spent many years helping people decide if marriage was for them, and then preparing them for it and supporting families after the fact. But to be clear, my marriage did not end because we didn't do our best to practice the Ingredients written on these pages. Rather, it ended because no one is invincible and sometimes there is enough pain, hurt, and certain other elements that make a relationship impossible to keep going in a way that is healthy for everyone involved. No one starts a serious, committed relationship with the intention of ending it. So, no matter what, it is hard on everyone. I know many good people who have found themselves in a similar situation. Yes, often relationships end because of decisions made that hurt others or that have serious ramifications, even if it is not on purpose. But often it is due to external factors as well that put unexpected stress on relationships such as accidents, health issues, death, loss, extended family, financial hardship, and so on. So, what advice does a guy whose marriage has ended have to offer about relationships?

Friends, like Sien, Kamar, and my cousin Rene, reminded me that those experiences help us learn and grow if we choose. Sadly, more fruit often comes from our hardships than from our successes. But I am also so much more than those painful moments. At times we all will be faced with that tough decision of whether we continue trying together or, for the good of everyone involved, it is time to part ways. My friends reminded me that despite what I've been through, I continue to work on myself as a person. I've not given up trying to be the best father I can be, and we've both committed to being the best co-parents possible as well. Furthermore, I have education and professional experience in this area, and I have the deep, rich relationship experiences of being a son, a brother, and a father of six. I have been a spouse, an employee, a boss, an educator, an athlete, and a coach, and I will always remain a student. So, thank you again to my friends who encouraged me. If you believe your experiences to be true growth opportunities, and if you know that our identities are often most clearly formed by learned lessons in life — then read on!

If you have a significant other, consider reading together or at the same time so that you can discuss what you're reading. Hopefully you'll be on the same page!

One more thing before we get into this book: I need to send a shout-out to Jason Silva for affirming my need to write. Many of you might know Jason from his major online presence and *National Geographic* show. Jason happened to be in my current home base of Kelowna, British Columbia. He was speaking at an event, and I had a chance to meet him. Our conversation surprisingly happened in the washroom, of all places. It was ironic, funny, and yet natural. I knew we'd cross paths again after that. However, listening to his talk and Q&A session confirmed for me that I needed to write this book and contribute to this conversation hopefully on a global scale. You see, during his talk Jason's focus was mostly on the things he talks about in his work such as advances in technology, where our species is headed, psychedelic experiences, and so on. Yet when people asked questions, so many were asking about Love and relationships.

I think he may have been as surprised as I was sitting there listening to how many people were concerned with this topic, since it was not the theme of his talk. However, it was a clarity moment for me... *Despite our undoubtedly amazing advances as a species and in technology, these advancements have not made relationships easier. Most people would probably agree that technology has likely made our relationships harder. Either way, people are still left with the desire to both understand and experience more fulfilling relationships. So, no matter how smart, how advanced, and how amazing we are, relationships are at the centre of our humanity. I aim to keep my writings short and to the point because I believe when it comes to most subjects "less is more," especially when it comes to words. Also, while my writings are clearly inspired by many people I've studied, encountered, and listened to on my journey, they are also rooted in historical, philosophical, and spiritual traditions as well as the writings or words of some of the voices/figures that I feel are contributing to relationships — this necessary reality of life. Where possible, I have footnoted for your reference.

Chocolate-covered French fries, anyone? Let's go...

Chapter 1

#1 RULE: IT'S ALL ABOUT YOU...

I chose to make the first chapter about this idea because it was the hardest Ingredient for me to learn. It may seem a little counterintuitive at first glance. If you are someone who studies self-improvement and participates in trying to make a difference, then this #1 Rule sounds like I am encouraging the selfish, individualistic part of our culture which many feel is destroying us. Well, I am not, so please allow me to clarify.

I once had an amazing family of origins counsellor named Lorraine who I thank for hammering this concept into my being. She journeyed with our family for a couple of years and really helped me to understand how my past impacts my present. The Ingredient I learned was that if I am bothered, upset, frustrated, angry, etc., it is mostly about Me and NOT the other person...* This can also apply to the positive if I am happy, excited, etc. Now don't get me wrong: this does not excuse people or their part in anything. For instance, for conflict to exist, it generally requires both people to make it continue. However, when we are triggered enough to engage in conflict, generally it is because of something in us that requires our attention.

I'll give you a gentle or simple example of this concept. One day I was in church listening to a pastor preach. As I was sitting there, I found myself getting worked up in my mind about what he was saying. The funny thing is, I knew that my kids who were sitting with me or those who were sitting around me did not know what was stirring inside me. I started to think "I can't believe this is what he chose to talk about" as I looked around at the people nodding off and the demographics. I continued for a good five minutes in my head of building steam while saying, "What a missed opportunity. Maybe that's why the Church is dying." These thoughts raced through my head.

Then I caught myself (thanks to the spiritual journey I've been on), and I stopped and said to myself: "Wait, why am I so bothered right now at what this man is saying? He's really just doing his job, or what he thinks is best." Then I remembered the Ingredient: it was about Me!* So, as I sat there self-reflecting, I realized that the part of my ego that always felt the need to be right was trying to show its ugly head. So, in that situation I was able to take a breath as I sat with my ego, and I was able to remind myself that maybe I don't always know what is best. Maybe there is actually a message not only in the experience I just had for me but in the pastor's words as well, so I should get back to listening!

When it comes to this concept, I have found the saving grace for me is often the Serenity Prayer. For those who don't know this prayer, it goes like this:

> *God grant me the Serenity to Accept the things I Cannot Change, Courage to Change the things I Can, and the Wisdom to Know the Difference.*

There is another portion of the prayer not known by most, so I encourage you to look it up. The words above are the most common part of the prayer that is recited by so many all over the world. It has become so popular because of 12-step programs like Alcoholics Anonymous. I think it is great that this prayer is so widely recognized because it speaks directly to the point I am making here.

We can only really control ourselves, although we often think we can control others, situations, or even outcomes. Yes, of course we can do our best to manipulate or even force others or situations which can affect certain outcomes we desire. But if we are doing that, then we are not in 'right' relationship with those people, or more so ourselves… Another great thing about 'The Program" is that the 12-step fellowships offer the chance to take a hard look at ourselves, our vices, our egos, our resentments, etc. Almost all spiritual traditions also have this embedded in them.

For example, in the Christian Gospels Jesus says, "Remove the log from your own eye first," or "go be reconciled with your brother or sister before you bring your gift to the altar." Ignatian Spirituality, Buddhism, and so on all call us to first examine what needs work in ourselves.

Of course, we can do things that fall under the basic laws of cause and effect. Just like traffic, or annoying ads in the media, when it comes to relationships, once we can accept that so many things are out of our control, like the reactions of others, then we can understand what is actually IN our control. Often it takes a little courage to change things that bother us, like how we "communicate" with others, or perhaps our lack of effort in that department, or even just being ready a little earlier to beat that traffic rush or choosing not to watch TV or even be online as much, whatever it is...

Notice I put the word "communicate" in quotation marks above because I want to draw our attention to that word. When it comes to relationships, we hear so much about communication. However, we tend to focus mainly on words, especially verbal forms of communication. We will touch on this issue in an upcoming chapter.

To wrap up this first Ingredient, I want to highlight two powerful sayings that crossed my path when I needed them. The first is a Buddhist saying I stumbled on in an unexpected book I was reading while flying home to Toronto a couple of years ago:

> *"The distance between wishing things were different and accepting them as they are, Is a tenth of an inch between Heaven and Hell."*[1]

---

1 Phil Jackson, *Sacred Hoops: Spiritual Lessons of a Hardwood Warrior*

This really hit me like a ton of bricks. I realized I had been going back and forth with so many things in my life, wishing they were different, and it was Heaven and Hell all the time. Once I came to terms with the reality that I sometimes need to accept things as they are, then I could choose my course of action or non-action vs. just reacting. Now the ball is in my court and I always have a choice.

The second saying goes like this:

> *"Yesterday I thought I was clever, so I tried to change the world. Today I am wiser, so I try to change myself."*[2]

I wish you all the peace of this wisdom that comes from understanding we can only change ourselves, especially when it comes

---

[2] Rumi (Poet).

#1 Rule: It's All About You...

to relationships. I've seen this firsthand so many times in my life. One example is that I am currently running a business with my mother. A few years ago, we would not have been able to work together. Granted, it takes two to have conflict, so she is responsible for her parts. But I experienced what happens when I change... everything changes. So that is why one of my favourite hashtags is **#bethedifference**. I hope you will too. I hope you will join me in contributing by reminding people that we can be the difference in our relationships, or we can at least try. Often it just takes one person to be first.

Let's continue looking for Ingredients...

Chapter 2

UNSUBTLE SUBTLETY

More than a few experiences inspired this chapter. Recently, I found myself in the presence of couples who were engaged in what I consider comfort-type behaviours. When people have been together for some time, subtle hints or ways of communicating often develop that are not subtle at all. They often make others who are aware around them feel quite uncomfortable... For example, I was at someone's house when the spouse arrived home from work. As they moved around the kitchen/living room, they kept repeating, "I'm hungry as a... (insert whatever animal you choose)." It was obvious to me, an outside observer, that they wanted the other person to get some food for them. Observing from a distance, I found this odd. I wondered why is it difficult for us to just come out and ask for what we'd like. Couldn't this person have just said, "Honey, I'm so hungry and tired. Would you mind heating up some food for me please?" Now, I'm sure I've been guilty of this type of unsubtle subtlety in my life as well, but it still begs the question.

Everything I write about can be applied to most, if not all, types of relationships. For example, some of my children are famous for asking leading questions like, "What are you doing at such and such a time?" and often, if I respond with a clear answer beginning with, "I'm busy doing…", I hear them say, "Ok, forget it." However, sometimes if I ask why, they will either follow with another leading question like, "Are you going in a certain area of town?", or "What time will you be done?" We both know that if they just came out and asked, "Could I get a ride to such and such a place, at this time, for this reason?", the conversation would save so much time and get down to the truth of the matter — and that's really what we want, isn't it?

I believe we do this in so many of our relationships, trying to subtly feel out the other person in the hopes that they will pick up our hidden messages and do what we would like... This is a type of manipulation we need to be careful of. So, the Ingredient of this chapter is as follows: when we think we are being subtle in hopes of getting what we want, we are often doing the opposite.*
It is better to simply say what we mean and let the other person freely choose their response, for then we are truly living the

ancient wisdom of being honest and fair to ourselves and the other person(s).[3]

I have a close friend who often does this without realizing it. It has become clear to me that they really value equal contribution in the relationship. However, this friend constantly drops hints like, "Why don't you bring (insert what you like) over this time to share?" Then often the truth will come out later if the conversation continues. They will say something more honest, like, "Since I always supply (blank), I think it's only fair if you do so this time." This is far clearer and more direct, although I don't recommend a "tit for tat" mentality. When we speak like this, then everyone can make their own choices regardless if we agree or not. Even if we don't agree, we may choose to do what is asked out of our love for the relationship because we know they value it.

---

[3] Don Miguel Ruiz, *The Four Agreements*.

Regardless, the important thing is that we have the freedom to choose.

My example of the friend above speaks to the underlying theme of Unsubtle Subtleties, which is really a disguise for Expectations.* I love the scene in the movie *Couples Retreat* where Vince Vaughn says, "The key is to lower their expectations of me, that way I can never disappoint them." This statement is funny in the context of the movie. However, there is truth in knowing that when we have Expectations, we often set ourselves up for Disappointment. The difficult task can be to become aware of our Expectations of the other person, why these Expectations exist, or where these Expectations come from.

Typically, Expectations* are rooted in our childhood/family of origin/cultural/life experiences. We are formed by what we've been influenced by and have seen examples of either growing up or in movies, music videos, TV shows, etc. So, the first step, though it can sound cliché, is really to acknowledge* our Expectations. Then we must ask ourselves, "Is it fair for me to have these Expectations of the other person(s) or myself?" Also, "Do I really Value these things, or have I just been conditioned that way maybe without even knowing it?" Only after contemplating these questions can we in fairness dare to be forthright about communicating our Expectations to the other person(s).

> **The last few sentences are a lot to take in, so re-read them a few times and take or make notes — these are crucial questions!**

Now remember that these things do not just apply to romantic relationships.

Things like Expectations can easily be applied to how we relate to anyone, including our sports teams, our classmates, our co-workers, and especially our family members! I believe if we have Expectations of others, then we should generally be willing to hold ourselves to the same accountability. Are we willing to do what we ask of others? This is also a positive responsibility. An important mentor in my life always used to say, "We have to want for others what we desire for ourselves too."

- Do you and I hold ourselves to the same measure as we hold others?
- Are we honest with ourselves about things under the surface we Value or desire, whether healthy or unhealthy?
- Are we willing to look at these Values and desires and sort out if they are worthy of holding on to or putting on to someone else?

- Are we willing to communicate honestly with those close to us about these things and why we even care so much about them?
- These sorts of questions are key to turning potential or real conflict into growth opportunities.

The next chapter is one of my favourites, yet it's a double-edged sword — especially because I happen to be writing this so close to Christmas!

Chapter 3

THE ART OF GIVING AND RECEIVING

Raise your hand if you have ever had the experience of doing something for someone and his or her response was not what you had hoped for.

Well, that's what this chapter is all about. The lack of joyful response from others is partially due to what we covered in the previous chapter — having Expectations, which, as we know, sets us up for Disappointment. However, the Ingredient to this has everything to do with understanding the art of Giving and

Receiving. We might address this a little more in the chapter on Passion, so for now let's focus mainly on Giving.

You see, one thing to remember is that we tend to Give in the way that we hope to Receive,* albeit this is often subconscious. It is rare that any of us would go out of our way overtly to actually give someone else what we want. But wait, this gets deeper. On the surface we only see things in plain sight. For example, if we like receiving gifts, then we may tend to give gifts. Yet the person we could be giving to may not care for these gifts unless they are just like us, which is also rare. Perhaps that person would prefer for us to affirm them in some other way such as by thanking them for helping around the house. If you're in a committed relationship, this could mean thanking your Husband or Wife, especially if kids are included in your family unit.

As with basically everything I write about or speak of, this can apply to many types of relationships, but in most cases, we see these things most strongly in our romantic relationships. In contrast, I want to once again offer the example of my relationship with my mother. She is someone who has always been next to impossible to buy gifts for on special occasions because she does not place much Value on "things." This is an admirable quality in a lot of ways because she is detached from material possessions, which as we mature is often the goal in life anyway. Instead, she really Values service or help. Someone like her has much more appreciation if I were to surprise her by doing a job that would make her life a bit easier.

These sorts of people can be harder to figure out for sure, but when we do, they love our gestures! So typically, we know from Gary Chapman, one of the experts or well-known authors in the field, that people generally Value service, affection, affirmation, or gifts, and I would add time. You can imagine in my family I not only have people like my mom, my sisters, and my extended family, but also my six children, even they are in a co-parent relationship with each other, my Ex-Wife, and I. It is a lifelong learning exercise to be in tune with what each person Values, because as we change, so do our desires (this topic will likely be a theme in Book #3!). Therefore, we must constantly try to be aware of how the people around us are growing too.[4]

Receiving, on the other hand, also touches on the first two Ingredients of this Recipe: It is All About You* and Unsubtle Subtlety.* You will find that the keys all tend to overlap or interface with each other. In

---

4   Garry Chapman, *The 5 Love Languages*.

this case, if we really know ourselves, then we can know what we desire, and better yet WHY we desire what we do. Furthermore, if we do away with the "subtlety," then we can articulate what we desire to the other person, which is all about **Receiving**. Now the goal is NOT to be selfish in asking for what we desire, but rather to be HONEST.

There is a big difference between "Honey, I really want the most expensive piece of jewellery you can buy me," and "Honey, if you're thinking of getting me a gift for my birthday, I would really love something that would make my commute to work more enjoyable." There is also a difference between "Mom, I want the newest iPhone for Christmas" even though the one they have is perfectly fine, and "Mom, my phone really doesn't have enough memory for pictures and I really love taking pictures; would it be possible for me to get some more memory?"

The Art of Giving and Receiving

The other side of Receiving in this sense is Gratitude.* If we can master the art of seeing the person's intention or thought, we will appreciate it, and so will they. Even with the greatest awareness, we will often miss the mark. Sometimes people will read what they think you desire the wrong way, even if they are listening. Perhaps we may not be communicating clearly, or perhaps their timing might just be off. For example, someone might prepare a romantic meal for you after finding out you've had a long or hard day. However, you might not receive it because you may just want to come home and curl up in bed, not sit in candlelight and talk about your long or hard day. Or you could walk into a situation like that and assume the other person's end goal is to have "action" in the bedroom that night when you are just not in the mood. Whatever the case, it goes back to **Rule #1: YOU or WE are the problem. If we cannot**

find a way to see past ourselves in order to appreciate the other person's good intentions,* then we need to find a way to get there.

As I mentioned earlier, this is one of my favourite topics, yet it is a double-edged sword on multiple levels, especially around times like Christmas, Valentine's Day, birthdays, etc. Nonetheless, it is a favourite topic of mine because Giving and Receiving are at the heart of expressing our Love for others. Yet is so easy to get this part wrong and miss the mark time and again... Raise your hand if you have a person somewhere in your life who is impossible to give gifts to, not because they Value service but because they have everything already... My father is that person for me. He wants for nothing and is content for the most part. It seems all he desires is for his kids to be healthy, stable, and good with each other. His wants seem fair and even noble at times.

While we naturally want to give to others on special occasions, we can only write so many heartfelt cards. Do you agree? Another edge to this sword is the Receiving piece, for to articulate what we desire we must first know it ourselves. This requires us to remember the #1 Rule again and take a hard look at why we want certain things.

On the surface, it could be that we are unhealthily materialistic at times. But on a deeper level it could be that we are looking outside of ourselves for joy and fulfilment from others or from "things." If this is the case, then we have to remember that we are responsible for our own happiness and that true joy comes from within, being right or good with ourselves, and our relationship with the Divine, whatever that looks like for you.*

The next question asks: What is your Foundation?

Chapter 4

VALUABLE FOUNDATIONS?

Back when I used to help couples prepare for marriage, I often opened up the process by asking if they could explain the difference between Values and Virtues. This pretty much always seemed to be a tough question for them. So, I ask you the same question: What do these words Value and Virtue mean for you? *Stop for a minute and see if you can actually answer this question for yourself.*

I'm asking because it is typically either one of these things that relationships are built on but sometimes, just sometimes, it can be both. Being conscious about it I believe is where the fruit is. Even if we do not realize it, we are usually operating out of one of these powerful influences.

One way to begin talking about these powerful influences is by focusing on Objective vs. Subjective motivations or influences. In my opinion, Values fall on the Subjective side and Virtues fall on the Objective side. Values are relative to whoever the person is. For example, most of my life I have really Valued watching basketball on TV, but some people in my life over the years would have preferred to not have any televisions in the house at all. You see, Values have so much to do with a person's past that they bring to the relationship and the things that are influencing them now in the present, of course. So, most of the time you have two people with very different backgrounds bringing a lot of different experiences to the table.

Virtues, on the other hand, are Objective in the sense that we all have both the capacity within us to access or exercise them as well as the capacity to aspire to them. Many things are Virtues; they are one of the few things that truly span across all traditions whether spiritual or secular. From a professional standpoint, a sounder understanding of Virtues is one of the things I have my Ex-Wife to thank for — other than being the Mother of my Children, of course. But back to the topic, one of the most popular sayings is "Patience is a Virtue." Yes, this is true, as are so many other things like love, peace, joy, charity, forgiveness, flexibility, self-control, and so on. Depending on which tradition you approach them from, they appear in many different forms — human Virtues, theological Virtues, cardinal

Virtues, etc. The point is that whether we choose to exercise Virtues or not does not make the reality of their existence a question; therefore, Virtues are Objective.[5]

This chapter is titled Valuable Foundations because we have to ask ourselves: What is at the core of our relationships? Now, of course this is going differ in different scenarios because a boyfriend-girlfriend relationship is not going to be the same as a parent-child relationship. However, one thing I have come to embrace is that although we may think our situations are unique, they really are not — the human condition is the human condition. Therefore, we say our experiences are similar but not the same... So, I am asking: Do you choose to build your relationships on Value or Virtue?*

---

5 The Virtues Project.

Valuable Foundations?

In my opinion, a relationship built on Value will be forever in flux because our Values change all the time. Therefore, when people say Compatibility is the cornerstone of a relationship, I believe it is a myth! For example, I was always socially aware when it came to Justice issues, but I never used to really pay much attention to Eco-Justice. Then, at one point in my young adult life, my eyes became opened to things like the privatization of natural resources that should be available to everyone, such as the owning and selling of water. This sparked a fire in me to avoid buying or drinking bottled water for a long time in order to raise my voice against this industry. Now I still drink bottled water from time to time, but I am more likely to drink tap water. In Canada we are blessed with one of the cleanest supplies of water in the world.

So why do I mention this example of what I came to Value? If I had been single at that time and someone had come into my life romantically, it may have caused some difficulty. I know it's a small example, but a lot of people like to only drink bottled water. You can transfer this example to things like dogs, working out, politics, etc. If either of us had based our relationship on Values, then the other would have to fit into that vision for us to really work. However, if instead I focused on a higher standard that is not attached to my personal preference, such as Justice (which applies in the water example), then this would free me to look for someone who aspires to similar Virtues. Even if it is expressed differently, at least we can have an appreciation of why the other cares so much rather than it being just about taste, preference, luxury, privilege, and so on.

Valuable Foundations?

It also allows the freedom that each does not necessarily have to care deeply about what the other cares about (within reason of course) in order for them to work because the relationship would not be based on Values. As I mentioned, Values, like the water example, have shifted for me slightly over the years but are still important to me as issues. I may just not be as zealous all the time. Therefore, I can still Value the Virtue of Justice without placing the fate of my relationships on a specific like water or hiking (in my opinion). Understand that we are always evolving. Those higher things we place importance on vary for everyone but can lift us up all the same.

Now you may disagree with me and say that relationships should be based on Values. And I would say that is perfectly OK as well, if that's what you choose. Remember what I said above, that the important thing is being conscious of what you're choosing to operate on. But another Ingredient in this part of the Recipe is that Disagreeing is OK.* When we understand that we all Value different things and aspire to different things, then we can be our own person and, with Respect (Virtue), agree to disagree sometimes. For our relationships to be healthy, that has to be OK!

I can't close this chapter without speaking on Love. Some people might be surprised I am not devoting a whole chapter to this but I actually have to write a whole book on Love and how Spirituality is so intimately connected (pun intended)... So, stay tuned; it is coming in the next book. What I will say for now is that Love is complex, as we all know, but in my opinion, it is often misrepresented in our Western "developed" world where I live. So is the concept of Time, but who knows? Maybe that will be the topic of another piece of writing.

*Love is a Virtue, and it is therefore available to all of us to give and receive. Love is one of the things inherent in our nature and connected to the Divine presence within (for those who believe). *Love is a lot of things, like a verb/action word; it is NOT a feeling! *Love looks different to all kinds of people, which I explain partially in Chapter 3. On the most basic level, if you desire Love, then you have to give Love too, and if you think you're not getting Love, maybe re-read Chapters 1-3. But sadly, I blame Hollywood for much of the confusion with this powerful word, just saying.

Keep your eyes out for the next book on *Love and Spirituality: The Double-Edged Sword* that it is!

Chapter 5

PASSIONFRUIT

We finally get to one of the exciting things in relationships that most people want to talk about — Passion! Now, Passion is clearly most applicable to romantic relationships; however, we can stretch Passion to apply to the thing(s) that make any relationship exciting, intriguing, and desirable, though these are typically only attributed to the beginning of any relationship. The title and inspiration for this chapter come from a favourite artist of mine and fellow Canadian — Drake. Part of the lyrics go, "...seeing you got so ritualistic..." He says a lot more in the song that seems relationship-driven to me, but for our purpose this is enough to focus on. I'm sure that if I asked you to raise your hand if you've ever been in a relationship that became ritualistic or routine and consequently you lost interest, most people would raise their hand very quickly.

This can even apply to a child of any age starting a new school year in the excitement of having a new teacher, classmates, or classroom. We all know how quickly that excitement or passion fades away in a school year. I think that the parallel with romantic relationships is self-explanatory and all too common. Sadly, this experience usually leads to breakups.

As a solution (or at least an Ingredient for your Recipe), I want to turn to one of my favourite authors/speakers — Esther Perel. In her book that she is most well-known for, she suggests that "passion exists in the space between the self and the other.*"[6] She offers a lot of really deep insights, and I highly recommend reading her book that is full of rich content. She highlights the traditional belief that we typically trade passion and excitement for stability and security when we get into a serious or long-term relationship. I think she raises the question ever so eloquently: Does it have to be that way, or can we possibly have both in a relationship? This is central for what we are cooking here.

The key Ingredient in Perel's statement above is the *space*.* Perel is proposing that for passion or excitement to live, there must be space. What does this *space* mean? Is it physical, mental, emotional, or what? I would say all of the above. In some cases, physical space can be a blessing in so many ways. For one, it forces us to have some

---

[6] Esther Perel, *Mating in Captivity*.

separation. Therefore, we must be good with being alone or by ourselves, which is the greatest challenge for most of us.

Of course, physical space can bring about other concerns such as trust issues about being apart from the other person, but that is a different issue which goes back to the last chapter. Do both people Value the Virtue of honesty or not? Now, just having physical space is certainly not enough to create or sustain passion in a relationship. However, if we can be good alone or being with ourselves, then we are achieving Rule #1. We are being responsible for our own happiness and understanding that other people should only add bonus happiness. Therefore, as a "whole" person without the need of anyone else to fulfill us, we can truly give to another person without any strings attached.

It is so important that we be "whole" on our own, because as soon as we are looking for another person to fill a void or something missing in us or in our life, we create dependency, which typically leads to co-dependency. There is a reason why Co-dependants Anonymous exists like so many other fellowships in regards to substance, eating, gambling, and sex. We do NOT want to be in co-dependant relationships with anyone — not our partner, not our siblings, not anyone. This tends to happen when we either lose ourselves in the other person or somehow develop a sense of responsibility for the good in their life. Co-dependency often leads to enabling perpetuating behaviour in the other person, and that is usually destructive!

Maintaining passion, newness, or excitement is the other element I mentioned

I might touch on. Well, here we are: it comes back to being able to give and receive. You see, for the previous couple of generations, since counselling or couples therapy has become a popular or necessary thing, in my observation there has been a fairly consistent approach from those advising people. They will almost always tell you that if you fix your communication and conflict resolution, then generally everything else would follow.

> On a side note, I often mention to friends that there is some belief now that couples therapy can increase the likelihood of divorce up to 75% from the already high general rate of about 50%. Of course, there are other factors to this. It is not that therapy is bad. However, often there are no guarantees that the counsellor/therapist is "for" marriage or

committed relationships, nor do they specialize in this area.

Of course, we would not know unless we ask, which people do not often do going in.[7] Another facture is that therapeutic problems require therapy.* Therefore, most people need to first go individually to deal with their own issues, and then the couple can hope to come together if they are both being responsible for themselves (Rule #1) and achieve some common goals.

Back to what I was saying, there are some voices finally proposing other ideas, and Esther Perel is one of the major voices. They are suggesting that perhaps we need to fix other things first, like our Intimacy, and then

---

7   Lee Baucom, Savethemarriage.com

everything else can follow. Intimacy has to do with the core of our being. Now Intimacy does not necessarily mean 'sex' — just to be clear...

One way to break down Intimacy is 'into me see,' which of course does involve our sexual nature but also so much more of what makes us who we are. Hence, this is why I mentioned earlier that we cannot discuss Love without discussing Spirituality too.

If we can get down to an intimate level with ourselves and those we are in relationship with, then we can do Chapters 2 and 3 really well. Finally, I want to name some aspects that round up the goal of having Passion in our relationships. If we can operate on an Intimate level, then we can *give, receive, ask, take, enjoy, trust, challenge, risk, and relish in so many beautiful things. You can apply all these to the bedroom, the boardroom, or the classroom — now there's a great recipe for Passion, I say!

Chapter 6

BITCOIN THAT LASTS!

I was recently very interested in watching what's happening with Bitcoin and the cryptocurrency revolution. It amazes me how much worth we people, our economies, and our governments put on emerging industries like this that are almost entirely all speculation. Their value is based on both the scarcity or availability and how much worth people are willing to place on them.

One of the questions with emerging trends like cryptocurrency is whether or not it will be sustainable (in every sense of the word), but mostly will it stick around or be simply a flashing trend? I am not going to debate the merits or pitfalls here, but I feel a parallel exists and is growing with our relationships, so let me explain...

I really need to speak to my fellow Men right now first for a couple of reasons (but Women — take note too). One, we Men love to find the next gold rush: that next big discovery that will make us rich and thus enable us to conquer the mountain of economics. However, sadly in the same breath, it seems we Men are rarely the ones who will invest in our relationships. I would estimate that in all my years of working with families and couples, 90% or more of the time it is the Women only who are looking for resources to invest in their relationships.

The problem is that those relationships include us and it does not work well — or at all —when only one side invests. Much like in world currency, you have to have people on all ends: buyers, sellers, and regulators. Men, I have been on a low-key quest to figure out why, other than the stereotypical responses like, "It's just the way Men are raised." We are so absent when it comes to this. I have my theories, and the main one involves the "Fatherless Generation." This does not mean that it only applies to Men whose fathers were absent in their lives; rather, it is a whole cultural problem.

My take on this theory is that a couple of generations ago, when we experienced all the recent 'revolutions' post-World War II such as the National Independence Movements, the Sexual Revolution, Feminism, Technological, Capitalism/Free Market, etc., that time was a flashpoint for social change which rapidly changed the defined roles that Men and Women had clearly been living prior to this period. Therefore, it has become extremely confusing what being a Man, or a father, looks like these days. This I believe even applies to fathers/pastors as well as any Men in leadership positions like teachers, coaches, etc.

So, with an abundance of things like absent fathers and single mothers, the rise of Women in the workplace, and Men increasing in the home, I believe we have a culture now where Men for some reason have thrown their hands up and said (subconsciously mostly), "We do not know how to navigate all this change and uncertainty." So, we are going to either do nothing about it, abdicate our place, or coast along in our relationships. Otherwise, we will simply focus on making money and that is the only success we will really care about — at least, that can be the message we send! Remember, this is my theory based on my education in religious, social, and cultural history and my own research and experience, so take it as you will.

The whole point of this last chapter is the idea of investing in something that we may not be able to see or fully understand. Also, we may not see the fruits of our investment anytime soon, but we will have to trust in the process. Believe me, it is hard to take my own advice just as often as the next person. I look at relationships in a very similar way. We need to ask ourselves most of the same questions as we would when making investments.*

- **What is it worth to me and the other person(s)?**
- **Is it sustainable? What would make it be sustainable?**

- **What makes it contain or keep Value to us?**
- **How much are we willing to invest in good faith?**
- **How much research will we do to be good investors?**
- **Who will we seek advice from in these matters?**
- **Who are the experts in the field?**
- **Who do I know that has done it and been successful?**
- **Who has failed or had unfortunate turnouts, and what I can learn from them?**

I propose when we look at relationships with questions like these, it is easier to see the parallel here.

One of the other similarities I see between currency and Love is that you cannot really see what you are investing in, i.e. the stock market or blockchain (crypto). Earlier I compared Love and Spirituality because I believe they are related in a similar way as I am saying here. Love is definitely the main Virtue that we express, access, or exercise in relationships. But no one sees it until someone actually uses it or shows it off — much like Spirituality and just like the stock market — otherwise, it is just speculation!

With currency, it remains only an idea that appears on a ledger or in an account record unless it is withdrawn or put to use in some way... But as promised, I am not going to get into Love here because it deserves a book on its own which is the next project! So, for our purposes now, I just want to highlight its importance since the goal of this book is to give practical applications to real-life situations in all types of relationships. Regardless, Love runs through all these chapters from loving ourselves to loving others, of course.

My challenge to us in this chapter is... can we view our relationships as something in which we cannot anticipate whether or not the risk of investment will show the return we want? If so, are we willing to invest anyway? The answer is up to each person; trust me, I wrestle with this concept daily. There are some key voices that I believe are worth recapping because these people are doing their part to contribute to a positive culture of relationships in their respective areas, and sometimes challenging the status quo while doing so.

Among those speaking to the general public and appealing to no specific spiritual tradition, gender, or ideology are Esther Perel, The Gottmans, The Chapmans (Gary), Lee Baucom, John Gray, and Brene Brown.

These are just a few I consider experts in this field. I strongly encourage you to look into their writings and speaking events; I am sure you will find an abundance of helpful material. Of course, in any spiritual tradition there will be writers and personalities addressing this. For Christians, especially, it is a very popular topic. I encourage you to dig into whatever you consider your belief system, whether Christian, Buddhist, Muslim, or whatever, and see how that material interfaces with this book.

Either way — I hope we can all choose to invest!

Epilogue:

ROWING LIKE CHRIS ROCK

It may seem odd that I am wrapping up the topic of relationships by mentioning comedian Chris Rock. I used to actually quote him often in the life coaching/spiritual guidance work I did. I feel he is one of the comedians who speak about real life (as they experience it), but often, at least from what I've found, his stories are about relationships. So, I want to recall just a couple of things I will paraphrase as best I can; I apologize to Chris if you are reading this and I get anything wrong.

"You can't have two different types of people together it won't last. For example, you can't have one who wants to do drugs and the other who wants to go to the library. You need two of the same types at least otherwise one will be out trying to get a hit all the time while the other will be saying let's go get a book."

"Women have an easier time saying No because ever since you were 13 every man you've met has been trying to sleep with you. But Men we are only as good as our options; some have more than others. Therefore, we can run away but if it chases us we can't run that fast."[8]

---

8 Chris Rock, *Bigger & Blacker Live*.

I only offer two jokes here as a sample, but there is a lot of rich material in his routines. Of course, he is making light of some serious relationship issues such as being in relationship with an addict. Obviously, this is no light matter. But it serves a purpose here of opening the conversation to Compatibility vs. Chemistry. I will address this in my blog and in the next book, so stay tuned. I just wanted to preface it here since I hope ours will be an ongoing relationship between Reader and Writer.

The second joke speaks to the stereotype that Men struggle to be faithful when presented with an opportunity to be promiscuous. In my experience, these sorts of examples, though humorous, are also very true and sometimes we just need to acknowledge them to shine light or speak truth into what is real. Then we can be aware and vigilant of our part(s) in these situations. This ultimately takes us back to the beginning of this book and the #1 Rule — remember?

Finally, the 'Rowing' part of this chapter's title refers to a saying I heard once that goes as follows,

> Life is a like Rowboat: we can't see where we are going, only where we are and where we have been. We have to trust the map we have chosen to guide us and perhaps the help of others in or outside the boat.[9]

Ultimately, we do the best we can with what we have been given. Yes, we can always do better or try harder and hopefully this book inspires someone to that end. When what we have been given fails us, we

---

9 Unknown.

must look elsewhere for help. So, the Final Ingredient* is not to avoid doing anything but to take what we have been given and find ways to make it better and sustainable or to heal what is needed.

I wish you the best in building your own Recipes for relationships... and as for chocolate-covered French fries...

I can say now that I have tasted them and they are delicious... Happy Cooking!

FOLLOW THE BLOG
www.kevinkishor.com
Contact me to book coaching sessions or speaking engagements via email at info@kishorventures.com

www.ingramcontent.com/pod-product-compliance
Lightning Source LLC
LaVergne TN
LVHW091935070526
838200LV00069B/1794